I0053287

WHAT OTHERS ARE SAYING

"Jane Moughon has written what all business owners seek, a guide to look at specific areas of our businesses that need tweaking to improve our profit. Jane's many years of advising owners of various types of businesses has equipped her with insights not processed by many. And, importantly, her style of writing is quick and easy to read. She can show you where to look."

William (Bill) Sherrill, Founder, and Chairman Emeritus
Wolff Center for Entrepreneurship
Bauer College, University of Houston

"If you need to cross a minefield, it makes sense to follow someone who has crossed it successfully. The same applies to business, sports, and life. I followed coaches to get me to the Olympics, guides to climb Kilimanjaro, I consulted an expert before I ran with the bulls in Pamplona, and specialists to build my businesses. This book will be your guide to help you avoid the pitfalls in business so you can save time and be more profitable."

Ruben Gonzalez, Olympian, Author Speaker
http://FourWinterGames.com

"This book is a real eye-opener for everyone who works in or owns a business. I encourage you to assess what's going on where you work to see if your company is at risk."

Dayna Steele, CEO YourDailySuccessTip.com

35 Silent Business Killers

How to Stop Them Before They Kill Your Business

Jane Moughon, M.S.

Copyright © 2016 Jane Moughon

All rights reserved. No part of this publication may be reproduced, stored in a retrieval system, or transmitted in any form or by any means—electronic, mechanical, photocopying, recording, or otherwise—without the prior written permission of the publisher and copyright owner. The only exceptions are brief quotations in printed reviews.

WORLD WIDE
PUBLISHING GROUP

7710-T Cherry Park Dr, Ste 224
Houston, TX 77095
(713) 766-4271

Published in the United States of America

Ebook: 978-3-9602-8680-6
Softcover: 978-0692743614
Hardcover: 978-1-68411-010-0

Introduction

Starting a business is easy. Making it successful is the hard part. Every year, more than 400,000 new businesses open their doors in the U.S. That sounds like a lot, until you consider that roughly another **470,000 businesses shut their doors each year**. That's right, in recent years, the U.S. – the land of the self-made man (or woman) – has been losing businesses left and right.

Most businesses shut down for pretty predictable reasons. Owners retire, companies are sold to competitors, or they can't adapt to a changing market or get a toehold in an existing one. It's a natural cycle of birth and death. Most of these enterprises shut down quietly, and their owners and employees move on to other ventures.

But some companies aren't content to simply fade away. Every so often, a business goes "south" in a dramatic fashion. Often, these failures seem to come out of nowhere, when **a once-thriving company suddenly goes belly up.** In other cases, ambitious new products or businesses are launched with great fanfare, only to sink suddenly.

In our search for reasons why companies fail, the following list was researched and compiled:

- Companies fail **due to unethical practices and management error.**
- Some fail **due to poor management—lack of a mission/goal and poor internal communications.**

5

- They fail **to innovate** and change with the times.
- Others fail to identify the correct national or international market segments.
- Failing companies don't keep up with technological advancements or adapt to changes in the market.
- Failure to do market research and commit to effective advertising.
- Not recognizing the importance of company personnel and compensating appropriately.
- Some companies don't realize the importance of adequate cash flow.
- Inadequate financing.
- And many others reasons.

Management involves leadership for dealing with complex issues, and *leadership* involves helping others deal with change. The maxim is truer than ever--particularly in today's 24-hour global markets in which your customers and your competitors can come from anywhere.

Change or die. To do this, you're going to need some good direction. Unfortunately, more often than not businesses fail to adapt. Even massive companies from 1985 have gone defunct.

In fact, only 71 companies remain today from the original 1955 Fortune 500 list. With the speed of technology adoption and a fast-paced global economy, companies rise and fall faster than you can say Alibaba.

So **what's the secret sauce to success** (or more accurately, survival)?

First, a **strong corporate culture** is key. But in addition to a defined **"perfect employee blueprint,"** creating an **innovation culture** and the ability to market solutions before your competitors can is a difference-maker.

In our experience, there are several reasons for stifled innovation:

- Fixating on one successful offering without accepting something better that can (and will) come along
- Only focusing on the customer of today without anticipating their needs for the future
- Failure to update technology and change with the times

This book is different. It's intended to serve as a wake-up call. Don't be fooled by how it's easy and quick to read.

Take time to assess your company. Read each section, ponder it and ask yourself, is this happening in my company? Ask your leadership team, managers, front-line supervisors and most importantly your employees if any of these things are visible or hidden in our own business.

There's a reason this book is titled "Silent Business Killers." Policies, procedures, processes, being slow to change, slow to make decisions, complacency, and certain attitudes creep in ever so slowly. One day you wake up and find your company is following the path of Blockbuster, Enron, Circuit City, DeLorean, MySpace and others who are now "business history." The question now is: What's Your Next Step? I trust this book will be a helpful guide.

Dedication

I dedicate this book to…

- Entrepreneurs who want to start businesses.
- CEO's and management teams currently running businesses.
- Every employee of all businesses, organizations, churches, and non-profits.

My intent is productivity, profit and success for all.

"Denial does not solve the problem. Denial does not make the problem go away. Denial does not give us peace of mind, which is what we are really seeking when we engage in it. Denial is a liar. It compounds the problem, because it keeps us from seeing a solution, and taking action to resolve it."
-- *Bill Kortenbach*

"Not since the digital revolution in the early '90s has technology placed such a comprehensive burden on business, employees and individuals to reinvent their business plans, services and products, and themselves to keep pace with the changing marketplace."
–Simon Mainwaring

Acknowledgements

Thank you Farell Moughon, Bill Sherrill, Marla Regan, Tracie Chancellor, Donna Mayes, Merlyn Fance, Grace Gonzalez, Eddie Smith, Tina Marie St. Cyr, Robert Olszak and others who gave input and encouragement as I wrote this book.

About the Author

Why are some people successful in business and some are not? Why do some businesses fail? In business, there are winners and losers.

Jane Moughon offers 35 things that if ignored, can cripple or kill your business. Discover what they are now. This is a wake-up call and a must read for everyone who owns or works in a business. Business is changing rapidly.

Easy to read. Easy to understand, Easy to apply format, you can take stock of your company and see if any of these 35 Business Killers are lurking. Don't let your business be another casualty.

Author, Speaker and Business Coach with over 30 years of business experience, Jane Moughon is an entrepreneur, former professional recruiter, Certified Coach with a Master's degree in Human Resource Management. Her company, RETAINAbility specializes in Employee Engagement, the Millennial Generation and the profitability of all companies.

Table of Contents

SECTION 1:
CEO's Responsibility

Killer # 1:
The Tower of Power

Clinging to an autocratic command and control culture that's slow to change doesn't work in a digital world. Keeping employees in the dark assures misalignment. The resulting confusion leads to wasted time, energy and resources—not to mention dysfunctional employees and costly remedial measures.

Transparency is the New
Top-Down Management Style

sincerity

fairness

clarity

openness

honesty

transparency

truth

believability

accuracy

directness

forthrightness

The concept is as simple as it is alluring. By making sure employees conduct their work in plain view—visible in open offices, monitored with sensing technology and tracked through digital activity, companies hope to increase accountability, collaboration, knowledge sharing, and innovation.

People Trust Companies That Are Transparent

Transparency produces trust. Who can trust a company or person who doesn't disclose information, and keeps everything close to the vest and, doesn't share anything?

"A lack of transparency results in distrust and a deep sense of insecurity."
– *Dalai Lama*

Killer # 2:
Sweeping Problems under the Metaphorical Rug

Failure to solve company problems and resolve ethical issues on a timely basis, or not at all.

Time is Money

Enron, once a sleepy natural gas pipeline company, grew to become the nation's seventh largest publicly-held corporation. But its shoddy business practices, aided by bankers and advisors feeding on the gravy train, brought down the company in December 2001.

"Just as character matters in people, it matters in organizations," says Justin Schultz, a corporate psychologist in Denver. The company's failure in 2001 represents the biggest business bankruptcy ever while also spotlighting corporate America's moral failings. It's a stark reminder of the implications of being seduced by charismatic leaders, or more specifically, those who sought excess at the expense of their communities and their employees. In the end, those misplaced morals killed the company while it injured all of those who had gone along for the ride.

When you keep sweeping things "under the rug" eventually you're going to trip from the mess you've made.

"It's fine to celebrate success, but it is more important to heed the lessons of failure."
- Bill Gates

Killer # 3:
Managing in the rear view mirror of life

Living in the past. Manufacturing false issues or problems and then attempting to solve them with old school methods that fail in a digital world.

Management is not up-to-date with the economic, cultural and technological times. The "Don't Fix What's Not Broken" mentality.

Don't Fix What's Not Broken......
Is Broken

Old adages don't apply to the fast-paced world of technology and business continuity requirements. It's certainly true that there are sometimes things that don't necessitate replacement, but we often put off replacing or fixing things due to our own complacency, being penny wise and pound foolish.

Consider Y$_2$K for example. On the morning of January 1, 2000, nothing happened. Very few systems around the world were affected. The reason why nothing for the most part happened is not because the Y$_2$K bug was overblown, but it was because IT WAS PROACTIVE AND IT DID ITS JOB. And I can assure you everyone was well aware that the cost of losing business continuity due to lack of proactivity would have been heads rolling in many organizations.

"Insanity: doing the same thing over and over again and expecting different results."
– *Albert Einstein*

Killer # 4:
Assumptive Leadership

Neglecting your single largest investment and assuming your people will just keep on giving and taking like any other machine in your factory.

Failure to realize your employees are the greatest of all your assets on your balance sheet.

Happy Employees = Happy Customers

One of the toughest corporate challenges is maintaining focus to stimulate desire and generate success in a large organization.

For example: Despite Southwest's size and success, its employees still give the impression that they are part of a small, aspirational effort. From its "bags fly free" policy to complimentary peanuts, it has resisted the paths other airlines have taken to squeeze more out of customers.

By keeping the important things simple and implementing them consistently, Southwest manages to succeed in an industry better known for losses and bankruptcies than sustained profitability. The airline is a vivid and rare reminder that size and success need not contaminate a company's mission and mindset, nor erode the addictive enthusiasm of management and staff.

The trifecta is this: happy, high-performing employees, happy customers, and stunning business results. If you're like the most successful firms, getting there means aligning your reward systems with your customers wants and needs – and ensuring that your desired outcomes are clearly defined, and everyone is held accountable for their results.

"Employees are a company's greatest asset. They're your competitive advantage. You want to attract and retain the best, provide them with encouragement, stimulus, and make them feel they are an integral part of the company mission."
- Anne C. Mulcahy

Killer # 5:
Believing the business impact of the millennial generation (born 1980-2000) will blow over and go away... if you ignore it

The implications inside organizations as to how work gets done are just starting to create ripples. More important are the bigger ripples that are being created as Millennials leave organizations and start to compete directly with their old employers.

The very same capabilities, skills, knowledge and desires that make Millennials desirable as candidates can also make them dangerous to an organization.

The "It-Will-Blow-Over-Thinking" Will Blow *You* Over

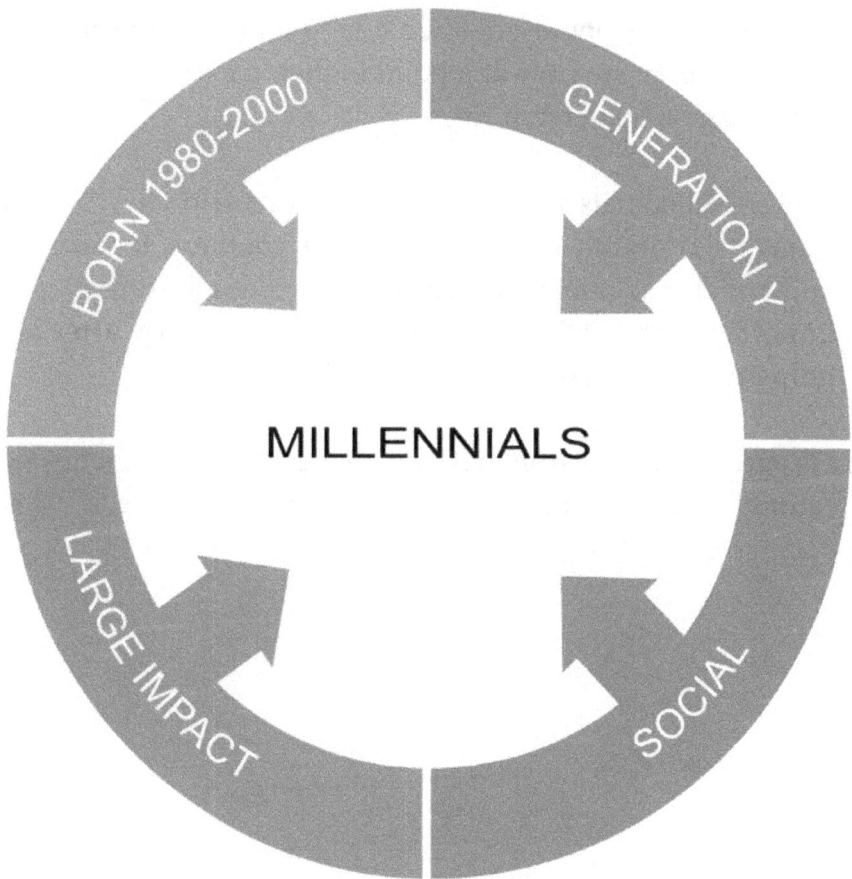

Every 20 years or so, there is a generational shift in the workplace. The most recent group — known as the millennial generation — is currently integrating itself into the workplace. And by integrating, they are making a seismic statement. Recent studies show that Millennials now make up approximately 25% of the total workforce and that by the year 2020 they will comprise almost 50%. Given that this generation is generally defined as those born between 1980 and 2000, they are now at a point in their careers where they are taking on leadership roles.

The Millennials are here, and they are here to stay. As their numbers continue to grow and they continue to take on additional leadership positions within your business, it is important not to take them for granted. They are, **after all, going to become your succession plan.**

"Progress is impossible without change, and those who cannot change their minds cannot change anything."
- George Bernard Shaw

Killer # 6:

Not reinventing your company, products, markets, add-on services, goals and dreams after original business goals are met.

Life Cycle of a Business is ignored.

Burnout

The product/service lifecycle is exactly as it sounds: the stages products and/or services undergo throughout their lifetime. These stages are introduction, growth, maturity, and decline. Each stage requires different actions and produces different results. In the end, you're left with a product that either continues to be relevant in the market or one that must be phased out due to technological advances or changes in consumer demand.

Those companies who carefully analyze the lifecycle of their products and/or services are more likely to continue having a major presence in an ever-changing market. Those who don't, however, may find themselves struggling just to keep their doors open. Consider following the advice mentioned in each lifecycle stage, and you'll be on your way to continued market relevance and business growth.

The key to redesigning organizations is acceptance of responsibility for leading yourself. Upgrading perceptual awareness and regulating your responses is fundamental. Without these and other skills, neither entrepreneurial leadership nor inspired innovation can vault over systemic barriers.

A whole scale shift in worldview is underway. It calls forth more from each person and invites company's willing to risk growth, to step forward.

"If it doesn't challenge you, it won't change you."
- Curiano

Killer # 7:

Having a boss who does not (or rarely) communicate or interact with line management or the employees.

Public Sharing of Excellence

A non-communicative manager can be a real problem, but not an insurmountable one. While part of any supervisor's job description includes effective communication with his or her staff, managers are rarely promoted because of their people skills. Many bosses are superb in dealing with complicated tasks but mediocre or poor in their day-to-day interaction with their employees.

Typically, professionals who have little communication with their bosses tend to think the worst. They wonder why their manager is avoiding them. The key to modifying his behavior (and yours) lies in asking for what you want.

Most people in technology spend more time at work than with their families — we're all familiar with that particular truism. And yet it all too rarely shapes the way companies do business.

Create a culture where people feel rewarded and valued. That means making sure people have interesting challenges and feel appreciated by their management and peers. It's making sure people feel ownership of what they are working on.

"Management is nothing more than motivating other people."
- *Lee Iacocca*

Killer # 8:
Management by Announcement or Decree

Thinking the employees understand, know what to do or how to implement on their own and will produce by "decree" or policy without personal buy-in.

How to Stay Out of the ER

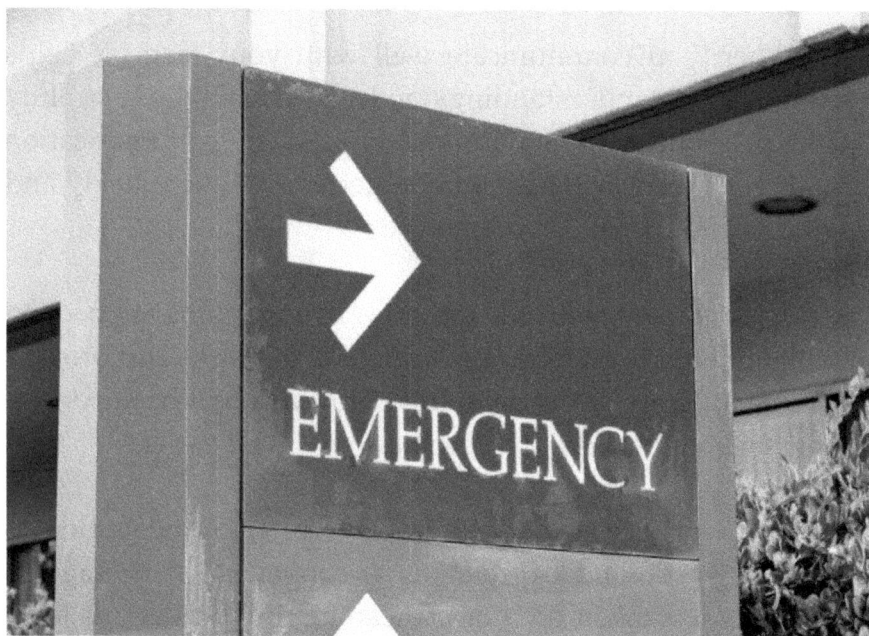

It is imperative in a leadership role that you communicate effectively. An age old aphorism goes, "It's not what you say, but how you say it." Communication is what separates a poor leader from an exceptional one. Having effective communication skills is the key to good leadership.

When you communicate well with your team, it helps eliminate misunderstandings and can encourage a healthy and peaceful work environment. Efficient communication with your team will also let you get work done quickly and professionally.

The moment you get the lines of communication open with your team, the process of carrying out tasks and projects will most likely go by smoothly. Plus you will be surprised how meeting targets will become a whole lot easier.

In a world where emojis (pictographs) are beginning to replace words and expressions -- conveying a message to someone has taken on a new meaning. Public settings have become a little less chatty and it's not uncommon to find rows of people in the bent-neck, plugged-in posture. Very little human-to-human communication, no eye-contact, minimal speech.

Perhaps we should put down the electronic devices and try the old-fashioned method of face-to-face communication.

"If you treat people right, they will treat you right, ninety percent of the time."
- Franklin Roosevelt

Killer # 9:

Not having a corporate cause or social responsibility program for employees (especially millennials) to help and support.

Millennials Without a Cause

American consumers value companies they believe demonstrate a commitment to corporate social responsibility, according to a new survey by the insurance company Aflac.

That's especially true for millennials: About 66 percent of millennial respondents said they are likely to invest in a company well-known for its corporate social-responsibility program, compared with 48 percent of adults older than 34. Eighty-two percent of millennials are likely to seek employment at a company recognized for its ethics, compared to 68 percent of people older than 34.

Millennials consider themselves civic-minded and active participants in today's world, and that it's up to them to assume the responsibility of making a lasting, positive impact on the future. Millennials have surpassed simply wanting help in supporting causes and are starting to demand that others, especially companies, do their part.

"Millennials embody the shift in today's workplace. They are motivated by a desire to transform themselves, their colleagues, and the world around them. If companies want to build engaged and productive workforces, they will need to find a way to tap into the millennial outlook."
- *Sean Graver*

Killer # 10:
The company's technology, website, and social media are not up-to-date.

Make New Super-sonic Social Friends

Technology is inescapable. It pervades every facet of our life. From how we work, play and live our lives, technology has created a revolution that will grow for as long as humans continue to advance in their capabilities.

With as many people on the internet today, with more and more coming online every day, keeping ahead of technology is a necessity if your organization anticipates long-term stability and growth.

If an organization continues to resist progress and decides not to keep up with technology, they are likely to fade away into obscurity.

Social media is booming, and it certainly shows no signs of slowing down. Sites like Facebook, Twitter, Pinterest, and Google+ allow brands to share information and increase customer engagement on a whole new level. Luckily, you have lots of ways to stay on top of the latest social media developments, though the best way to learn will always be to dive in and try it for yourself.

"We don't have a choice on whether we DO social media, the question is how well we DO it."
- Eric Qualman

Killer # 11:
Transparent, upward/downward and sideways company-wide communication system is not in place.

Prevention is the Best Cure

Perhaps the most important part of a good manager's job is communicating effectively. Creating a culture of communication in which managers and employees share common goals and work together to meet them can boost a company up and even save it from the gutter. It is important to understand the importance of communication, especially in difficult times or during times of change.

Timing is critical in letting employees know about upcoming changes in order to reduce uncertainty. You also need to be very clear about your purpose when you meet with them.

Successful employers know that in order to feel engaged, employees need to see what's happening at their organization. Do your best people understand company goals? Do they know how well the company is doing? Do they understand the organization's biggest challenges?

If you're not keeping your people in the loop, your corporate transparency could use a little work.

"There has never been a better time for people in business to reconnect through meaningful communication to what matters most to them and to each other for the greater good."
- *Miti Ampoma*

Killer # 12:

Customer service and customization of products and services is not the company's number one priority.

Add Value, Under Promise and Over-Deliver: Public Sharing of Excellence by Creating Customer Loyalty

CUSTOMER SERVICE
☐ Excellent
☐ Very Good
☐ Good
☐ Average
☐ Poor

At Zappos, our higher purpose is delivering happiness," said Hsieh. "Whether it's the happiness our customers receive when they get a new pair of shoes or the perfect piece of clothing, or the happiness they get when dealing with a friendly customer rep over the phone, or the happiness our employees feel about being a part of a culture that celebrates their individuality, these are all ways we bring happiness to people's lives."

Most presenters fail to make the distinction between selling and inspiring. According to Hsieh, a brand is a shortcut to emotions. Decide what emotion you want your brand to stand for. "Ultimately, it causes people to be more attached to the brand and the company. You'd much rather support a company that inspires you than one that doesn't," says Hsieh.

When customers feel taken care of they are more inclined to buy from you again.

Since studies have shown that it costs 6 to 7 times more to acquire a new customer than keep an old one, outpacing your competition depends on having a loyal tribe of happy customers.

"It takes months to find a customer ... seconds to lose them."
- *Mireille Ryan*

Killer # 13:

Not changing your corporate culture to embrace the change brought by the largest workforce, the Millennials.

Turn the Ship Without Sinking It

Employees who understand your mission statement and can express "the why," will be more inspired and engaged. It also helps boost company performance--among other benefits.

At the heart of any company is it's mission. A business' mission defines what it stands for--its purpose and the reason for its existence. Mission declares the difference a company seeks to make in the world. A strong mission is lofty, ambitious, and sometimes audacious.

By providing this strategic direction, mission-driven leaders maximize employee engagement as a key driver of organizational performance–and as a strong predictor of business success.

While the times and your company's employees are changing, it is important that not only the younger employees need to be understood, but also, the more senior employees need help understanding and embracing the change. It is important to consider how your company will embrace, manage, promote, and retain, these new, highly technical workers because Millennials are not going away. They will only grow in the workforce.

"Whenever you see a successful business, someone once made a courageous decision."
- *Peter Drucker*

Killer # 14:

Not standing out from your competitors by offering career opportunities to attract the top talent that every company wants.

Left Behind

A 2015 report from LinkedIn surveyed more than 10,500 workers who had changed jobs and found that 59 percent of respondents did so because of better opportunities and a stronger career path. For a bit of perspective, only 54 percent took a new job because the compensation was better.

For employees, the ability to grow and continue on their career path is extremely important. They're waiting for employers to show them how they can do that within their current company. Ask employees where they need assistance to help them define their career paths.

Everybody has their own goals and expectations for their career. Unless employers discuss this with their employees, it's near impossible to be a part of that growth.

To ensure that your company gets the first pick from the candidate pool in your community, examine your hiring policies. Is your company standing out from your competitors by having a streamlined hiring process that provides applicants with a clear idea of what your workplace is like? If not, think about incorporating some or all of the above suggestions, and hopefully your company's pool of top-tier candidates will increase.

"If you aren't a little different than your competition, you're in trouble."
– *Mark Sanborn*

Killer # 15:
Biggest KILLER of All…Believing that most or none of these KILLERS are true since you can't see them on your financial statements.

Denial – The Mother Ship of Silent Business Killers

When you look at your workforce today, what do you see? Employees actively engaged in their job and the success of the organization? People in management positions effectively leading their people and delivering sustainable results? Is turnover kept to a minimum? Is the organization leading your industry? If so, congratulations. You need to consider yourself and your organization fortunate.

If you look at the reality of what's happening in the workplace today, Gallup, having tracked employee engagement for 30 years, reports less than one-third of employees are engaged at work. More than half are not engaged in their jobs, and nearly one-fifth of employees are actively disengaged.

It's time for organizations to recognize that valuing employees must come full circle. Their people are their most valuable asset in securing the future.

If you're in business, you simply must keep accurate accounting records. But beyond that -- remember, perfection is a myth -- the "out-of-sight-out-of-mind" mentality does not apply here.

"Denial does not solve the problem. Denial does not make the problem go away. Denial does not give us peace of mind, which is what we are really seeking when we engage in it. Denial is a liar. It compounds the problem, because it keeps us from seeing a solution, and taking action to resolve it."

- Bill Kortenbach

Section 2:
Leadership Team
Responsibilities

You can't do it all yourself, although you may want to. You may even feel like you have to. But unless you have a strong team at the top, you and your company will struggle under the weight of growth. Knowing how to select, manage and lead a Top Team is one of the secrets to growth.

A great Top Team extends the values, vision, mission and plan throughout the company. It aligns the company and accelerates its growth. A dysfunctional team can tear a company apart and send it down the tubes.

To build a great Top Team, be wise about the people you hire and promote. Scrutinize your high-level candidates as if you were hiring your own replacement - because you are. Look for people you trust. Hire people who can handle new duties that you delegate, and who will follow-through to completion. Insist on people who use good judgment, treat others with respect, and meet or exceed performance expectations.

"Teamwork is the ability to work together toward a common vision. The ability to direct individual accomplishment toward organizational objectives. It is the fuel that allows common people to attain uncommon results."
– *Andrew Carnegie*

Killer # 16:
Compensation and benefits plans are less than your competitors or the market

Conduct a Compensation Check

An organization may choose to offer a compensation package that is valued less than packages offered for a similar job in the labor market. An employer with a "lag the market" philosophy is likely to be at the back of the line when it comes to hiring and retaining employees, especially those with special skills. These problems are the direct result of below-market pay.

With the Internet providing pay information with a click of a mouse, employees are less willing to stay and support an organization when they know they are underpaid. Good employees may leave while less-skilled employees may stay with the organization.

Turnover is very expensive! It is estimated to be at least six months' pay for a non-exempt (hourly) employee and one years' pay for an exempt (salaried) employee. No organization wants to be a training ground to groom employees for its competitors. (See Turnover cost list in the resource section of the book.)

Employers who want to succeed in this increasingly competitive environment must have a well-designed compensation plan that motivates employees, controls compensation costs, and ensures equity. The best compensation plans mirror the culture of the employer. Therefore, employers should establish a compensation philosophy. Benefits programs should also be part of an employer's compensation strategy.

"The purpose of a compensation system should not be to get the right behaviors from the wrong people, but to get the right people on the bus in the first place and keep them there."

- Jim Collins

Killer # 17:

Failure to put programs and processes in place to minimize employee turnover, and discover all the real and hidden costs of high turnover.

Know your True Cost of Turnover

Employee turnover cost is usually defined as the cost to hire a replacement employee and train that replacement. Often the training costs are only those to get the new employee productive, but they should include all the costs of getting the new employee to the same level of productivity as the employee who quit.

These costs include both direct costs like the fee paid to a recruiter to find candidates for you as well as indirect costs like the business you lost because you didn't have the capacity to handle it all while you were short-staffed.

Generally, the higher your turnover rate, the higher both your direct and indirect costs will be. And as the turnover rate increases, the costs will increase faster. (See the list of turnover costs we've identified in the back of the book.)

High employee turnover hurts a company's bottom line. Experts estimate it costs upwards of twice an employee's salary to find and train a replacement. And turnover can damage morale among remaining employees.

"Today's market is incredibly competitive in every industry around the globe. The difference between success and failure is talent, period."
- Indra Nooyi

Killer # 18:
Only relying on "Exit" interviews to discover problems that need fixing in your company.

"Stay Interviews" are more effective

Stay Interviews are designed to get specific information by asking the right questions of your high performing employees. These interviews will bring to light their individual challenges and offer you an opportunity to make the necessary changes at your company so that these employees stay for the long-term.

Stay interviews offer you a chance to find out the reasons each employee is, and wants to be, productive at your organization. Having a regular Stay Interview program demonstrates to your employees how much you value them because you're careful to ask and listen to why they are still with your company.

When is the best time to do a stay interview? Experts recommend doing them at least once a year opposite the employee performance review, and twice in the critical period during which your company experiences attrition of new hires (for example the first 40-50 days for fast food, or 90-180 days for engineers).

"We can't stop employees from leaving unless we have a plan to make them stay."
- Talent Management Institute

Killer # 19:
Hiring and Keeping employees who create drama or have bad/negative attitudes.

Surgery Protects Negativity and Drama from Spreading

Drama, drama, drama! It's all around us, but it can be especially noticeable in the workplace. Drama in the workplace comes in many shapes and forms: Constant complaining about other employees; long-winded discussions about personal relationships; inappropriate outbursts in the office. Unfortunately, this can create uncomfortable situations and can even result in a hostile workplace environment. So the question is, how do you create (and maintain) a workplace environment with no drama?

One of the most effective ways to prevent or remove drama in the workplace is to catch it early. It would be good to attach to your employee handbook a detailed addendum that clearly defines office drama and the company's policy for handling it. It would also be productive to send positive internal communication and address these policies at company-wide staff meetings.

Negative employee attitudes and less-than-professional behavior can poison the workplace atmosphere.

Complaint forms, personnel files, performance reviews and disciplinary warnings should be in place and legally compliant. Programs like different punishments for the repeated fights; nipping negativity before it derails morale; and investigating even seemingly frivolous complaints should be considered to prevent or mitigate negativity and drama.

"A bad attitude is like a flat tire. If you don't change it you'll never go anywhere."
- *Frompo.com*

Killer # 20:

Failure to keep track of turnover by each supervisor and by each department to discover potential problems.

Decoding the Silent Killers:
Departmental MRI's

"Well, now we know what not to do."

An analysis of employee turnover data can help pinpoint why employees are leaving your organization and what you can do to retain the best.

Even better, the results will help you proactively join your organization's decision makers in their struggle to achieve quality and profitability.

Departments with high turnover may require HR attention. Supervisors with high turnover may need management training. And positions with high turnover may need to be restructured to be more interesting.

High employee turnover can have a severe impact on your business, both financially and emotionally. If you suspect that turnover is an issue for your business, you should take steps to recognize possible causes of turnover, measure your turnover rate, determine turnover costs, and then address your turnover problems. Be able to recognize the signs of what causes turnover, whether they be conflict, discontentment, monetary or other.

It costs the business money every time an employee leaves because it takes, even more, resources to return to the same level of productivity or level of performance that you had before.

"A bad manager can take a good staff and destroy it, causing the best employees to flee and the remainder to lose all motivation."
- *Unknown*

Killer # 21:

Offering very little or no Supervisory/Management training and especially "millennial employee" management training.

Employees leave their Boss,
not the company

People leave managers, not companies. In short, the central relationship between manager and employee plays a critical role. Beyond that, other factors also contribute. These include belief in senior leadership, pride in one's company and the chronic uncertainty resulting from a steady stream of reorganizations, layoffs, and pressure "to do more with less."

But no matter the precise constellation of factors, which vary according to the character and circumstances of an organization, there's no question that a chronically high level of employee disengagement represents both a failure of management and a fundamental challenge to it: a challenge to do what is needed to keep vast numbers of individuals interested in their work, feeling good about their organizations, and working as productively as they can.

One very important responsibility of a supervisor or manager is to help your staff with their professional and career development. You can do this by providing opportunities for them to develop the knowledge, skills, abilities, tools, resources, and opportunities to be successful in their job and career. Examples include providing on-the-job training and coaching, giving them performance goals and feedback, asking about and supporting their development goals.

"Treat employees like they make a difference, and they will."
- Jim Goodnight

Killer # 22:
Allowing or Not Recognizing Workplace Bullying, Harassment or Abusive Conduct

Stand Up Together and Leave No Place for Bullies to Hide

Bullying is "repeated, health-harming mistreatment by one or more employees directed toward another employee that takes the form of verbal abuse, threats, intimidation, and humiliation, interference with work production or in some combination." It is a form of abuse. It is recognized by the National Institute for Occupational Safety and Health (NIOSH) as a non-physical form of workplace violence.

Business leaders should care because of its impact on employee health, work productivity impaired by excessive absenteeism, turnover (loss) of the best and brightest workers, workers comp and disability claims and litigation expenses. They should care, but those same national surveys found that the most likely response by employers to reported bullying was to ignore or worsen it.

Workplace bullying is often hard to identify and is often unnoticed and unaddressed until it leads to more devastating consequences.

On-the-job bullying can take many forms, from a supervisor's verbal abuse and threats to cruel comments or relentless teasing by a co-worker. And it could become the next major battleground in employment law as a growing number of states consider legislation that would let workers sue for harassment that causes physical or emotional harm.

"Whenever one person stands up and says, 'Wait a minute, this is wrong,' it helps other people to do the same."

- Saveours Schools

Killer # 23:

Failing to have clear job duties, responsibilities and career path plus a system for measurement of performance and progression.

Brightly Light the Way

In earlier generations of workers, an unspoken, sink-or-swim approach to on-the-job training was often good enough to bring new employees up to speed. Yet that approach might be less effective with those from the Millennial or Generation Y demographic, a group raised with different expectations and work styles.

Millennials, possibly more than any other generation, require clear direction, guidance, and goals from their managers.

To leverage the talents of this highly educated and goal-oriented generation, companies need a new approach. Rather than assuming that new workers will absorb an organization's culture without explicit discussion and while proceeding just as their elders have done, enlightened companies are re-designing supervisor and leadership training to accommodate the more interactive and collaborative work styles of Millennials.

Consider implementing a process that begins with writing out detailed descriptions for each role and what it takes to excel in it, and ends with the design of a performance evaluation "cycle" (setting goals jointly, evaluating progress against those goals, then making decisions and recommendations based on that progress).

Organizations that are fair, consistent and transparent in the way they train, support, evaluate and promote their employees benefit from higher morale and thus greater productivity and improved recruiting success.

"If you are working on something exciting that you really care about, you don't have to be pushed. The vision pulls you."

- *Steve Jobs*

Killer # 24:
Appreciation and Gratitude for Your Employees are Almost Non-Existent

Teach Gratitude, the Soul of Success

Successful companies are proving that employee happiness sets them apart in many ways from their competitors plagued with employee apathy and turnover. Happy employees are more productive, loyal, and positively contribute to a company's financial goals—impacting the bottom line.

Competition for recruiting top talent is fierce. Savvy companies attract the best people when they treat employee relationships like customer relationships—as if the business depended on it.

If one of your customers complained about your product or service you would quickly react, consider the potential impact on your sales and brand, and address the issue to keep the customer from leaving. Companies with the most successful cultures are those who respond similarly to an unhappy employee.

If you want your employees to be happy and productive, you need to give them recognition for a job well done and let them know their work is appreciated and important.

"Appreciation can make a day, even change a life. Your willingness to put it into words is all that is necessary."
- Margaret Cousins

Killer # 25:

Failure to set up a system for letting employees change jobs or move to different positions to learn first-hand many of the business functions.

Big Picture Thinkers

As Millennials grow within their current position, their talents and interests may begin to alter. Be open to restructuring their job or creating a new position for them in order to keep them engaged and learning new things. Otherwise, after a couple of years, they will be looking to jump ship.

Consider bringing in a junior person below them to train or manage, and look for ways that they can mentor or teach others at the company to strengthen their leadership skills.

Millennials are not quiet about what they want and if it is not available in your organization, they are not going to stick around for very long. You need to figure out how to motivate them in order to retain that young talent.

Employees usually feel more engaged when they believe that their employer is concerned about their growth and provides avenues to reach individual career goals while fulfilling the company's mission. A career development path provides employees with an ongoing mechanism to enhance their skills and knowledge that can lead to mastery of their current jobs, promotions and transfers to new or different positions. Implementing career paths may also have a direct impact on the entire organization by improving morale, career satisfaction, motivation, productivity, and responsiveness in meeting departmental and organizational objectives.

"Employees who believe that management is concerned about them as a whole person – not just an employee – are more productive, more satisfied, more fulfilled. Satisfied employees mean satisfied customers, which leads to profitability."

- Anne M. Mulcahy

Killer # 26:
Orientation/On-Boarding is boring and common.

Engagement Starts in the First Five Minutes

Employee orientation programs are much more successful when they are less about the company and more about the employee.

Unfortunately, a lot of companies do it wrong. Organizations will talk about recruiting from outside the company because they need new ideas and new blood, but then there is this tendency to shut off the new and basically transfer the corporate culture over to the new employee.

Previous studies have shown that employees are especially productive and happy when employers encourage them to use their individual signature strengths on the job, but historically those studies did not consider the employee onboarding process.

The researchers hypothesized that companies would see positive performance results by emphasizing employee individuality from day one, testing their hypothesis through a series of field and lab experiments.

Your new employee orientation is a make 'em or break 'em experience, for a new employee. At its best, the process of new employee orientation solidifies the new employee's relationship with your organization. It fuels their enthusiasm and guides their steps into a long term positive relationship with you.

Done poorly, your new employee orientation will leave your new employees wondering why on earth they walked through your door.

"There are only three measurements that tell you nearly everything you need to know about your organization's overall performance: employee engagement, customer satisfaction, and cash flow. It goes without saying that no company, small or large, can win over the long run without *energized employees who believe in the mission and understand how to achieve it.*"

– *Jack Welch, former CEO of GE*

Killer # 27:
Not having fun and social activities at work

Gamification is here to stay

"People rarely succeed unless they have fun in what they are doing."
- *Dale Carnegie*

Managers and leaders need to communicate often that it's okay to have fun at work, and they themselves should be having fun and joking around every now and then. It's important for employees (especially new ones) to see that this is okay.

First of all, this is incredibly important for the psychology of an employee, and is what's known as the "progress principle". It's important to recognize hard work and is one of the ways employees stay motivated. Use this as an opportunity to have a little fun. A positive company culture is critical for retaining employees.

Employees are coming to work either way, so why not make it more fun for them to enjoy? Why not make them excited about coming into work, so that they go above and beyond in their job?

Everyone is happier and more productive when they have fun together.

And what some leaders don't understand is that when people are not having fun, they're tense. Then as a result of the paralysis, they can't make decisions—and studies have shown that when you're paralyzed, you're incapable of being creative.

"The supreme accomplishment is to blur the line between work and play."

- *Arnold J. Toynbee*

Killer # 28:

Letting employee's skills, drive and motivation stagnate by not offering training classes

Not Up To Date

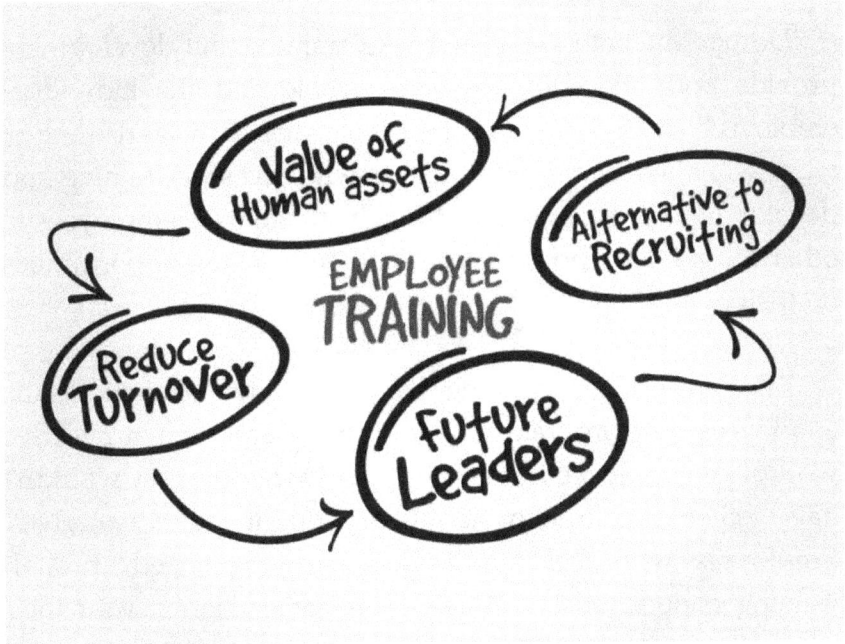

Training presents a prime opportunity to expand the knowledge base of all employees, but many employers find the development opportunities expensive. Employees also miss out on work time while attending training sessions, which may delay the completion of projects.

Despite the potential drawbacks, training and development provide both the company as a whole and the individual employees with benefits that make the cost and time a worthwhile investment. Employees with access to training and development programs have the advantage over employees in other companies who are left to seek out training opportunities on their own.

The investment in training that a company makes shows the employees they are valued. The training creates a supportive workplace. Employees may gain access to training they wouldn't have otherwise known about or sought out themselves. Employees who feel appreciated and challenged through training opportunities may feel more satisfaction toward their jobs.

Employee motivation should be one of the key objectives featured in any business organizational plan. It goes without saying that a motivated workforce is a more creative and productive one. Innovation is necessary to produce quality work. Only driven employees would put in the effort to find better methods to deliver quality output in the most efficient manner possible. The more engaged and motivated your employees are, the more it helps with reducing turnover. Those who frequently look out for better opportunities may be the ones with great potential while the ones who stay on could be just settling for their circumstances.

"Employees cannot become more productive in every sense of the word unless they are provided with continuous on-the-job-training."

- Gregory Balestrero

Killer # 29:
Departments withholding information and feuding with other departments creating departmental silos.

Collaboration and Team Work
Eliminate Silos

A silo mentality can occur when a team or department shares common tasks but derives their power and status from their group. They are less likely to share resources or ideas with other groups or welcome suggestions as to how they might improve. Collaboration in a business culture with silos among teams or departments will be limited unless collaboration benefits the members of the department.

The structure of a business itself, or the jobs that employees do in relationship to one another, can foster a silo mentality. If a business owner sets up her company into dedicated business functions and does not establish meetings, training sessions or policy-planning sessions that bring people from different departments together, they will stick to their roles, which can produce closed-mindedness.

A business owner must plan team-building and information-sharing strategies to help employees think more globally. The employees also need incentives to work together, such as a new project that offers a financial reward for interdepartmental collaboration.

Managers need to remember that motivation encompasses a wide variety of tactics including common interests, individual investment in growth, shared voice, and positive words of encouragement. All of the tactics related to motivation are designed to avoid the "it's not my job" attitude and encourage input, teamwork, and most importantly – productivity.

"The success of Teamwork: Coming together is a beginning. Keeping together is progress. Working together is success."

- Henry Ford

Killer # 30:
Having Unengaged Employees

Awaken the Sleeping Giants in your company

Having your top employees operating in a state of near-unconsciousness all day long can be a huge problem. After all, these are the people who are capable of performing the company's most valuable work. They are also the ones interacting most frequently with your internal and external customers.

They should, therefore, be driving the organization to greater and greater levels of profitability. Instead, they are often content to ambivalently toil away, unconcerned with whether they make a sale or exceed a customer's expectations.

It's concerning—and it should be. The overall health of your business enterprise is at stake!

When employees have poor attitudes toward their employers or do not feel empowered in the workplace, they offer less of their potential in organizational life. A critical question for both researchers and internal communication consultants to think about is—what engages employees, promotes employees' commitment to organizational goals and at the same time enhances employees' well-being?

"The employees must love the company before the customers ever will."
- *Simon Sinek*

Killer # 31:

Employees and departments are not working toward the company mission and goals.

Power of Team

Goal setting allows for a quicker execution of company strategy. Without good alignment to strategy, every bit of forward motion is a struggle.

With everyone working together towards the same objectives, your company can execute strategy faster, with more flexibility and adaptability. Essentially, goal alignment strengthens your leadership and creates organizational agility.

Your company's productivity and profitability can be directly traced to the performance of your employees working to achieve individual goals, which in turn, should be directly aligned to support broader company goals.

With top-down alignment, communicated throughout the organization, you increase everyone's ability to cover more ground, faster. It's the difference between pursuing a path together as a well-oiled machine or as individual parts flying off in multiple directions.

No employee is an island when it comes to accomplishing your company-wide goals. Most can be achieved only through the combined efforts of many people. By cascading and aligning goals across multiple employees, you can create a corporate atmosphere of shared responsibility that will drive the success of your company.

An automated performance management solution can greatly simplify the task of establishing these shared goals and help keep your entire organization working together toward the same objectives.

"The strength of the team is each individual member. The strength of each member is the team."

-Phil Jackson

Killer # 32:
Having Employees and Managers with Hidden Agendas.

Thinking What You Don't Know Can't Hurt You, Your Employees and Business?

Step back and look around your organization. Are the objectives of the organization in alignment with the intentions of its leaders? Or, is your company being led by hidden agendas that must be revealed in order for the organization to grow and prosper?

America's corporations don't have the time or the money to finance ineffective leadership. Don't allow tenured leaders to run on auto-pilot. Challenge their objectives. Ask questions. If not, opportunities remain unseen if corporations continue to operate blindly.

It's time for leaders shape up or get shipped out. The workplace today can't afford for anyone not to be completely focused, productive and steady at all times.

Employees want to believe that their leaders are focused on the betterment of the team. If this requires well-intentioned political maneuvering to advance team goals and objectives, then great. The same is true that Employers want to believe that their team members are focused on the betterment of the team.

However, if it comes across that a leader or team member is solely intent on protecting themselves and their own personal agendas – trust from the entire team will be lost quickly and is difficult to recapture.

"If you could get all the people in an organization rowing in the same direction, you could dominate any industry, in any market, against any competition, at any time."

- Patrick Lencioni

Killer # 33:
Not identifying your current superstar employees and training them to be your future company leaders.

Left Behind

Leadership is learned by practice, and reinforced with coaching and formal training. One of the biggest challenges facing today's integrators is identifying and training current and future leaders. Spotting a potential leader is fairly easy…easy, at least, if you know what you're looking for.

Keys to spotting potential leaders: They Attract Attention in the Workplace; they are Active in Meetings; They Are Thinkers; They Are Great under Pressure.

Before embarking on training and coaching, be sure to set clear expectations of what success looks like. Employees, and especially leadership candidates, need to know what we expect from them. The best ways to do this are to conduct regular meetings and facilitate consistent and frequent communication between managers and potential leaders.

Your next leader could currently be in a lower-level position at your company, and it may even be a job that doesn't really resemble the leadership role that you are trying to fill.

So, are you aware of those future leaders in your organization? The ones who could be doing great things for you in the future? Are you developing them? If you answered "no" to any of these questions, you might be overlooking a potential superstar.

"Leadership is lifting a person's vision to high sights, the raising of a person's performance to a higher standard, the building of a personality beyond its normal limitations."
- Peter Drucker

Killer # 34:
Not Putting Your Customers at the Center of Your Business

Good Customer Service = Successful Business

Unless your company has a stranglehold on your industry or was a first-mover, everyone agrees that in order to have a truly successful business, you need to have more than just a great product or service. Good customer service is the better half of a real successful business.

When we talk about successful businesses we don't mean just in terms of revenue, nor just traditional customer service, but successful in the sense of operating in the territory of positive sentiment -- so much that the mention of your brand triggers good feelings from a customer. Yes, when customer service evolves into the customer experience.

Follow Up

The simple step of following up a sale to ask what your customer thinks of your product or service will make them feel valued. They are also more likely to tell others about your business.

Generate Repeat Sales

Use every opportunity to tell your customers about sales, promotions and services you provide. Help your customer feel that they benefit by receiving preferential treatment and inside information from you.

Customer Appreciation

Most consumers appreciate personalized care and attention. Remembering your customer's name, or a previous interaction with them, helps your customer feel they 'belong' to your business.

Remember your customers and pay attention to their needs and interests. Customers today expect personalized, unified conversations across sales, service, and every other interaction with the organization - regardless of how big or small the company is. When sales and service teams work together, everyone benefits from a 360-degree view of the customer, providing a better experience for the customer.

"Your customers don't care how much you know until they know how much you care."
- Damon Richards

Killer # 35:
Not realizing that Cash is the Lifeblood of a Business

Out of Money = Out of Business

I'm always amazed when I run across Chief Financial Officers who don't believe a cash flow statement is the most important part of the financial package when it comes to small business management.

Small businesses run on cash and knowing where cash is and where it's gone is among the most important things a small business owner can know.

If you don't know what a cash flow statement is or don't think it's very important, here are some reasons you might want to reconsider your position on this topic:

- A cash flow statement can tell you if you're running out of money while you're profitable.
- A cash flow statement can tell you if the owner is taking too much money out of the business.
- You will see the results of building inventory, letting receivables grow or paying suppliers more quickly.
- Capital purchases show up as an expense.
- You'll see what your bank loan payments are doing to your cash. As with equipment purchases, payments to your bank for principal don't show up on your profit and loss statement.

These changes in your cash position often mean your business will run out of money if not managed properly. They have nothing to do with your profit and loss statement, but they have a huge effect on the cash in your business.

"Many accountants would rather face an angry barbarian horde than tackle their cash flow statement."

- Nicole Fende

Introduction Sources

http://businessinsider.com/10-brands-that-committed-suicide-2013-3

http://cheatsheet.com/business/5-big-name-businesses-that-completely-failed.html/?a=viewall

http://businesspundit.com/10-businesses-that-failed-to-adapt/

https://vocoli.com/blog/july-2014/10-companies-that-failed-to-innovate-and-what-happened-to-them/#sthash.zZPy9SSX.dpuf

Source Material by Killer Topic

Killer # 1:
Harvard Business School – Dr. Ethan Bernstein

Killer # 2:
Forbes – Enron Ethics and Today's Corporate Values

Killer # 3:
Zdnet.com article – If it Ain't Broke-Don't Fix-It Bad Advice

Killer # 4:
Bloomberg View: The Secret to Southwest's Success

Killer # 5:
Forbes – John Kotter – May the Millennial Force Be With You

Killer # 6:
Huffington Post – Stages of a Business Lifecycle

Killer # 7:
Career Cost – My Boss Has No People Skills

Killer # 8:
Small Business Trends – Communicate Effectively

Killer # 9:
The Chronicle of Philanthropy – Corporate Responsibility

Killer # 10:
Axis Technical – Keeping Up with Technology in Workplace

Killer # 11:
Blog E-Skill – Employees Engaged & Motivated

Killer # 12:
Business Week - Zappos Story – Delivering Happiness

Killer # 13:
Gallup Poll Business Journal – Why Company Mission Driven

Killer # 14:
Entrepreneur - No Career Path – No Retention

Killer # 15:
Business Paths –Employers Should Embrace Employees

Killer # 16:
Shrm.Org – Employee Compensation

Killer # 17:
Management.about.com – High Cost of Employee Turnover

Killer # 18:
Work Institute – Conduct Stay Interviews

Killer # 19:
My LLC – Creating a Drama-Free Work Zone

Killer # 20:
ASAE Center - Analysis of Turnover

Killer # 21:
Forbes – People Leave Managers, Not Companies

Killer # 22:
Workplace Bullying Institute - Bullying in the Workplace

Killer # 23:
SHRM – Giving Millennial Employees Feedback

Killer # 24:
Fast Company.com – Treat Employees Like Best Customers

Killer # 25:
Clickz Column – Millennials – How to Inspire Them

Killer # 26:
Forbes – HBS Working Knowledge – First Minutes of New Employee Orientation Critical

Killer # 27:
Office Evibe – Fun Company Culture – Good Business

Killer # 28:
Small Business Chronicles – Importance of Training

Killer # 29:
Your Business – AZ Central – Silos – Means Business Culture

Killer # 30:
Business.Com – Your Most Valued Employees Are Engaged

Killer # 31:
Success Factors – Goal Alignment

Killer # 32:
Forbes – Glenn Llopis – Leaders Must Reveal Hidden Agendas

Killer # 33:
Sound and Communication – Identify Future Leaders

Killer # 34:
https://salesforce.com/blog/2014/04/what-is-good-customer-service.html

Killer # 35:
http://stage2planning.com/blog/bid/35202/5-Reasons-Cash-Flow-Statements-Are-Important-KPI

Source Material with Links by Killer Number

Killer # 1:
http://wsj.com/articles/the-smart-way-to-create-a-transparent-workplace-1424664611

Killer # 2:
http://forbes.com/sites/kensilverstein/2013/05/14/enron-ethics-and-todays-corporate-values/

Killer # 3:
http://zdnet.com/article/if-it-aint-broke-dont-fix-it-bad-advice-can-break-your-business/

Killer # 4:
http://bloombergview.com/

Killer # 5:
http://forbes.com/sites/johnkotter/2014/09/11/may-the-millennial-force-be-with-you/

Killer # 6:
http://huffingtonpost.com/jackie-nagel/ignoring-your-productserv_b_7536264.html

Killer # 7:
http://careercast.com/career-news/my-boss-has-no-people-skills

Killer # 8:
http://smallbiztrends.com/2013/11/ways-to-communicate-effectively-in-the-workplace.html

Killer # 9:
http://philanthropy.com/article/Corporate-Responsibility/233668

Killer # 10:
http://axistechnical.com/the-importance-of-keeping-up-with-technology-in-the-workplace/

Killer # 11:
http://blog.eskill.com/employees-engaged-motivated/

Killer # 12:
http://businessweek.com/smallbiz/content/may2009/sb20090512_831040.htm

Killer # 13:
http://gallup.com/businessjournal/167633/why-company-mission-driven.aspx

Killer # 14:
http://entrepreneur.com/article/253123

Killer # 15:
http://businesspaths.net/Articles/16/employers-should-embrace-workers-as-valuable

Killer # 16: http://shrm.org/publications/books/documents/5_chapter3.pdf

Killer # 17:
http://management.about.com/od/money/a/The-High-Cost-Of-High-Employee-Turnover.htm

Killer # 18:
http://workinstitute.com/solutions/stay-interviews?gclid=Cj0KEQiAkIWzBRDK1ayo-Yjt38wBEiQAi7NnP1F0lc-cVgKlL1eh-4zEHf67d5QLtROPL_Ia7f1Ct28aAs168P8HAQ

Killer # 19:
http://myllc.com/mbp-creating-drama-free-work-zone.aspx

Killer # 20:
https://asaecenter.org/Resources/ANowDetail.cfm?ItemNumber=27085

Killer # 21:
http://forbes.com/sites/victorlipman/2015/08/04/people-leave-managers-not-companies/

Killer # 22:
http://workplacebullying.org/hriq/

Killer # 23:
http://shrm.org/hrdisciplines/diversity/articles/pages/whythemillennialgeneration.aspx

Killer # 24:
http://fastcompany.com/3032557/treat-your-employees-like-your-best-customers

Killer # 25:
http://clickz.com/clickz/column/2395967/millennials-aren-t-all-bad-if-you-know-how-to-inspire-them

Killer # 26: *http://forbes.com/sites/hbsworkingknowledge/2013/04/01/first-minutes-of-new-employee-orientation-are-critical/*

Killer # 27:
https://officevibe.com/blog/fun-company-culture-good-business

Killer # 28:
http://smallbusiness.chron.com/importance-training-development-workplace-10321.html

Killer # 29:
http://yourbusiness.azcentral.com/silos-mean-business-culture-3448.html

Killer # 30:
http://business.com/human-resources/your-most-valued-employees-are-unengaged-what-do-you-do/
Killer # 31:
https://successfactors.com/en_us/lp/articles/goal-alignment.html

Killer # 32: http://forbes.com/sites/glennllopis/2011/11/07/objectives-define-intentions-why-leaders-must-reveal-their-hidden-agendas/

Killer # 33:
http://soundandcommunications.com/identify-companys-future-leaders/

Killer # 34:
https://salesforce.com/blog/2014/04/what-is-good-customer-service.html

Killer # 35:
http://stage2planning.com/blog/bid/35202/5-Reasons-Cash-Flow-Statements-Are-Important-KPI

Source Material for Comment Pages

Killer # 1:
http://fastcompany.com/3036794/the-future-of-work/why-a-transparent-culture-is-good-for-business

Killer # 2:
via Funny Status.com

Killer # 3:
Albert Einstein

Killer # 4:
http://mcorpcx.com/do-happier-employees-really-mean-happier-customers/

Killer # 5:
http://businesswest.com/blog/millennials-and-your-business/

Killer # 6:
http://huffingtonpost.com/great-work-cultures/unlocking-the-key-to-rede_b_9321440.html

Killer # 7:
http://businessinsider.com/how-this-company-retains-95-of-its-employees-2016-2

Killer # 8:
http://huffingtonpost.com/marsha-pinto/stop-drop-and-talk-the-im_b_9307248.html

Killer # 9:
http://adweek.com/socialtimes/cause-related-marketing-millennial-mindset/142701

Killer # 10:

https://bluehost.com/blog/educational/how-to-stay-up-to-date-on-social-media-for-business-trends-2750/

Killer # 11:
http://parim.co/transparent-communication-building-business-relationships

Killer # 12:
https://helpscout.net/customer-loyalty/

Killer # 13:
http://redfusionmedia.com/managing-generation-y-millennials/

Killer # 14:
http://www.selectinternational.com/blog/attract-top-talent-in-a-competitive-market

Killer # 15:
http://www.entrepreneur.com/article/233168

Killer # 16:
http://www.blr.com/compensationtips/compensation-plan

Killer # 17:

http://guides.wsj.com/management/recruiting-hiring-and-firing/how-to-reduce-employee-turnover/

Killer # 18:

http://hiring.monster.com/hr/hr-best-practices/small-business/conducting-an-interview/stay-interviews.aspx

Killer # 19:

http://businessmanagementdaily.com/19426/bad-attitudes-complaints-handling-workplace-negativity

Killer # 20:

http://bizfilings.com/toolkit/sbg/office-hr/managing-the-workplace/employee-turnover-issues-tactics.aspx

Killer # 21:

http://hrweb.berkeley.edu/toolkits/managers-supervisors/helping-employees-develop

Killer # 22:

http://insurancejournal.com/news/national/2013/03/04/283420.htm

Killer # 23:

http://broadeducation.org/asset/1344-employeeevaluationguide.pdf

Killer # 24:

http://businessnewsdaily.com/8152-employee-appreciation-tips.html

Killer # 25:

http://shrm.org/templatestools/toolkits/pages/developingemployeecareerpathsand ladders.aspx

Killer # 26:

http://humanresources.about.com/od/orientation/a/orientation.htm

Killer # 27:

http://inc.com/jay-steinfeld/11-ways-to-make-work-fun.html

Killer # 28:
http://cleverism.com/motivation-employees-best-way/

Killer # 29:
http://forbes.com/sites/brentgleeson/2013/10/02/the-silo-mentality-how-to-break-down-the-barriers/#187be41a5f3e

Killer # 30:
http://instituteforpr.org/cost-unengaged-employees-inspire-change/

Killer # 31:
https://successfactors.com/en_us/lp/articles/corporate-goal-alignment.html

Killer # 32:
http://forbes.com/sites/glennllopis/2013/12/09/7-reasons-employees-dont-trust-their-leaders/#4525e27c1a20

Killer # 33:
https://calipercorp.com/future-leaders-right-front/?doing_wp_cron=1456537723.6354320049285888671875

Section 2:
http://entrepreneurship.org/resource-center/a-top-team-is-key-to-growth.aspx

TURNOVER COSTS

Actual Costs	Hidden Costs
Continued Benefits	Lower/Lost Productivity During Interim (Peers, Supervisors, Subordinates)
Recruiting Fees	Lower/Lost Productivity During Ramp-Up Time
Increased Unemployment Taxes	Resume Screening
Advertising/Marketing Materials	Interviewing Time/Expenses
Interviewing Costs	Informal Training
Assessments	Missed Deadlines
Criminal Checks/Reference Checking	Loss of Intellectual Property
Medical Exams/Drug Tests	Lower Morale From Overwork
Relocation Expenses	"Chain Reaction" Turnover
Temporary/Contract Employment Fees	Client Issues From Turnover
Orientation Materials	Client Loss
Training Programs	Company Reputation Cost
Separation Pay	Separation Processing
Accrued Vacation	

The Estimated Turnover Cost is 2.5 to 4.5 Times the Employee's Salary.

Jane Moughon   Millennial Specialist | Speaker | Coach | RETAINAbility.com
Email: Jane@retainability.com Web: www.retainability.com

Contact Page

Jane Moughon is available for a free consultation regarding the following.

- Speaker for your event or organization
- Lunch and Learns
- Workshops
- Breakout sessions at your conference
- Keynote Speaker
- Consulting
- Radio/TV Interviews
- Work-Ready Skills Certification Classes for Young adults at schools, churches, organizations, or for new-hires at your company
- Take our employee retention assessment on RETAINAbility.com

Call now 832-455-4579
Email: *Jane@retainability.com*
Sponsorships available

Get Your Free Report
10 Steps to Employee Engagement
at: http://35SilentBusinessKillers.com

www.ingramcontent.com/pod-product-compliance
Lightning Source LLC
Chambersburg PA
CBHW070725220326
41598CB00024BA/3302